BRITONS

"WANTS
YOU"

JOIN YOUR COUNTRY'S ARMY!

GOD SAVE THE KING

Reproduced by permission of LONDON OPINION

INTRODUCTION

At the time George V became King in 1910 there was much unrest in Britain. The army had been called in to contain rioting workers, the police were needed to restore order among the suffragette women, and in Ireland the clamour for home rule intensified. The new Labour newspaper of 1912, the Daily Herald, duly reported it all.

Nevertheless there was much patriotism. In March 1911 'All British Week' increased awareness of imported goods, and in June the King's coronation was held, with his son's investiture as Prince of Wales in July. There was pride also in Captain Scott's expeditions, though sadness when he died trying to reach the South Pole before the Norwegian Amundsen.

The unthinkable happened in 1912 when the 'unsinkable' Titanic hit an iceberg on her maiden voyage and sank with the loss of 1,513 passengers and crew. 'The peril in the air' was influenza – outbreaks reached their height in 1919. Lloyd George's health tax stamp was introduced in 1911.

The new dance crazes were the Tango and the Foxtrot; the popular pastime of picture-going made the front page of comics; and the latest doll mascots were Kewpie (above) from the USA and Britain's 'Fumbs Up'.

With the outbreak of war in August 1914 a new patriotism emerged. Anti German sentiment was fuelled by reminders of 'atrocities' in Belgium, of the bombardment of Scarborough, of Nurse Cavell being shot as a spy, and of the sinking of the liner Lusitania – torpedoed without warning and the loss of 1,195 lives.

The Great War was fought from trenches with machine guns, gas attacks, flame throwers, aircraft, submarines and tanks (a new mode of transport for Santa Claus). While women helped in the factories, 'mother's day' prospered, and those at the front sent millions of postcard messages home. But real news came from the new journals and tabloid press: the Somme, Gallipoli, Verdun, and in 1916 the Irish uprising in Dublin.

The Allies drew strength from the arrival of the US troops in June 1917 and peace came in November 1918.

ROWNTREE'S
High Class
CHOCOLATES
Makers to their Majesties
The King and Queen

George V became King in May 1910 following his father's death. On 22nd June 1911 his Coronation was held at Westminster Abbey. Souvenirs abounded; particularly favoured were the commemorative tins issued by confectionery manufacturers — towns and cities also gave these tins to their school children. The splendid souvenir hat was sponsored by Black Cat cigarettes. The Coronation Exhibition was held at White City, containing exhibits from all parts of the Empire. On its first day, 262,000 visitors attended. Fireworks were provided by Brocks who sold their firework tin (see opposite centre).

Weldon's Ladies' Journal APRIL 1910 3d

SEVEN PATTERNS GIVEN AWAY

FASHIONS for ALL

JULY NUMBER 3 PENCE

FREE PATTERN

FREE PATTERN

FREE TRANSFER

Weldons ILLUSTR
No. 417

Weldons Catalogue of Fashions 3d
Just Out

Weldon's Ladies' Journal 3d SEPT. 1910.

No. 375
Vol XXXII

Six Patterns Free
FOLDED SEPARATELY

An Artistic Coloured Plate and Transfer for Braiding Given Away

FASHIONS for ALL
JUNE 1913 3D

LEA
F

The decade opened with the hobble skirt and the heady hats of the Edwardian period, but there was growing controversy over the new vogue for women wearing trousers, referred to as the harem skirt, an influence from the orient. Women's emancipation was in the air. By 1915 the tubular style of previous years was giving way to looser fitting outfits that were less restrictive. The hemline began to rise to show off the ankle and by the end of the decade was still rising — to the excitement of many men. The fashion magazines, such as Weldon's Ladies' Journal, provided not only fashion tips and patterns (enabling many to create their own outfits at home) but also tips 'for the Hostess' and 'Heart to Heart Talks': 'no life is happy which is at the mercy of trifles'.

6

ARE THESE YOUR BAGS MADAM?

THE HAREM SKIRT

"LOOK HERE, MAUDIE — THESE TROUSERS HAVE JUST COME FROM THE TAILORS; ARE THEY YOURS OR MINE?"

The new money-saving Dress Paper.

HOME FASHIONS

SEPTEMBER, 1914

1d

Nightdress Pattern Free!

VERY EASY TO MAKE

on's 1D

O DRESSMAKER

NOVEMBER 1914

PATTERN of this BLOUSE
IN TWO STYLES
ENCLOSED in this COPY

COMING FASHIONS

La Mode de Demain

7D
NET.

"Viyella"

(Regd. Trade Mark)

Unequalled
for
Comfort
and
Durability.

FREE CHOICE of PATTERNS
See page 24

MARCH 1918
No. 457

DRESSMAKER

IS NATIONAL ECONOMY

Pattern No. 58237
SPRING BLOUSE

Pattern Inside
to make all these Styles
also a Transfer Design of Spray of Daffodils

H'S
CHILDREN'S
MAKER

LADY'S CAMISOLE and GIRL'S NIGHTDRESS PATTERNS GIVEN AWAY INSIDE
SEPTEMBER, 1916

The Camisole pattern, No. 14,213, is given away inside.

Pattern of Girl's Nightdress, No. 14,255, is given away inside. This smart Coat Frock pattern offered free in exchange for coupon.

No. 14,256.

OCT 1917
No. 460

4½D

Pattern No. 57389
Dress in two styles
and Fur Collar

Pattern No. 57399
Evening Dress

A Message to your Editress

WELDON'S

WELDON'S LADIES' JOURNAL

Easter No   Sixpence

Pattern No. 58441
Coat and Skirt,
post free 3d., with
Coupon on p. 23.

No. 466
APRIL 1918

DRESSMAKER

APRIL 1915

BLOUSE

KIRT and PYJAMAS

Weldon's Fashions

WELDON'S LADIES' JOURNAL

4D

Pattern No. 56749,
Blouse and Muslin Collar

Pattern No. 56748,
Skirt and
Over bodice

Pattern No. 56750,
Coat and Skirt in any
size, FREE, see p. 313.

Patterns Inside

A Dressy Frock, Morning Dress and Muslin Collar
also a Transfer Design of a Peacock, Suitable for Embroidery, Painting &c.

HOME FASHIONS

DECEMBER 1919

Patterns to make These 3 Frocks Inside

4½

Full directions for making these Three Frocks given inside.

FESTIVITY   FASHION   NUMBER

COSMOS LAMPS

COSMOS

WILL ALWAYS PLEASE

BRITISH MADE

B. FRENCH,
Electrical Engineer and Contractor,
EXCHANGE STREET,
KIDDERMINSTER.

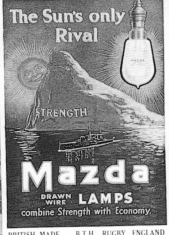

The Sun's only Rival

STRENGTH

Mazda
DRAWN WIRE LAMPS
combine Strength with Economy.

BRITISH MADE. B.T.H., RUGBY, ENGLAND

Sat. 4.11.18.25

THE "HUE" FIRE

A HEALTHY, NATURAL, CHEERFUL
& ECONOMICAL BARLESS FIRE WITH-
OUT THE DISADVANTAGES & EXPENSE
OF REMOVING EXISTING STOVE.

HOUSES IN METRO-LAND

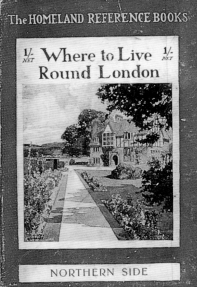

The HOMELAND REFERENCE BOOKS

1/- NET   Where to Live   1/- NET
Round London

NORTHERN SIDE

ENJOY YOUR READING WITH AN OSRAM

ELECTRIC COOKING
The Essence of Cleanliness
IS CHEAP HEALTHY CONVENIENT

ELECTRIC COOKING

COUNTRY HOMES IN METRO-LAND.

THE

O-S. WIRING SYSTEM

Look at my Electric Wiring!

"STAR" VACUUM CLEANER

PATENT No 18899/11.

The Light of every Home

JOHNSON, RIDDLE & Co. Cf. LONDON.

NDON,

CHEERFUL HOM

DOMESTI
HOT WAT
SUPPL

HOOVER

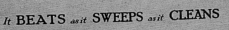

It BEATS as it SWEEPS as it CLEANS

OSRA
LAMP

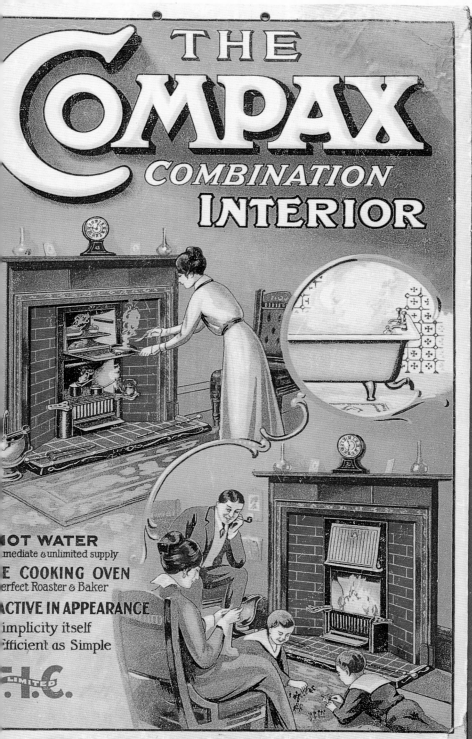

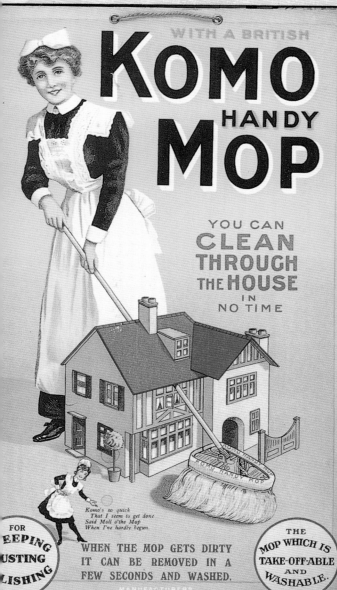

Suburbia was growing fast, particularly around London where it was dubbed Metro-Land. New estates were built with country outlooks — barn roofed houses in Wembley Park or mock Tudor homes in Bushey Herts, with 'two golf clubs near'. The Ideal Home Exhibition of 1913 (first held in 1908) had a 'labour saving' section where the Star vacuum cleaner of 1911 was demonstrated and sold for 30/-. In 1912 the Hoover electric suction sweeper arrived from the United States (the 1919 model is shown opposite). Electricity was the new wonder power, now being used for cookers — 'the essence of cleanliness, is cheap, healthy and convenient'. More homes had electric lighting, but at the beginning of the decade a proud house owner could still say with pride to her guest, 'look at my Electric Wiring!'

9

Traditional block soap for washing clothes was under attack from the new soap powders like Persil (launched 1909) and Rinso (1910), while liquid boot blacking sold in stone jars was being replaced by the less-messy solid boot polish sold in tins, such as Cherry Blossom (1903) and Kiwi (arriving in Britain from Australia during 1912). Two new brands, both launched in 1910, were the gravy browning Bisto (the Bisto kids first appeared in 1919) and Oxo cubes. A growing number of meat extracts in cube form appeared in shops at this time, including Allies Brand beef tea cubes. Amongst new brands in the boxed chocolate market, Cadbury's launched Tray and Milk Tray chocolates in 1916, both varieties had been sold loose from the tray during the previous two years. Tins had become a popular medium for souvenirs, filled with tea, biscuits or confectionery. Mazawattee tea produced canisters for the 1911 coronation depicting the king and queen (second shelf above) and

biscuit firms celebrated the event with Coronation varieties. For the Prince of Wales' 21st birthday in 1915 (opposite top left), Lyons' Tea celebrated with tea caddies. At the start of the Great War more tins marked the occasion with patriotic fervour - the allies' flags and army leaders were proudly pictured. Brands reflected the situation and sentiments: Needler's Military acid drops and Barker & Dobson's Tipperary toffee, Macfarlane Lang's Campaign biscuits and McVitie & Price's Homeland biscuits. Fry's issued a series of chocolate boxes each with an allies' flag. By 1917 some products were helping to save on raw materials; for example, cocoa for Bournville, Cadbury and Rowntrees (top shelf) now came in card packets rather than tins, and tins for meat cubes were replaced by card packs (such as for Oxo and Bifi on second shelf). To celebrate victory, Ridgeway's tea produced a 'Peace' canister (including USA flag) and Scott & Turner launched their Victory baking powder.

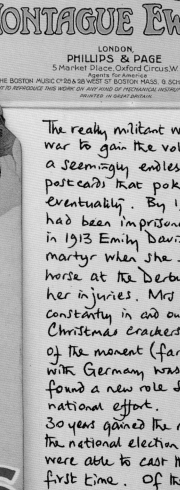

The really militant woman was waging war to gain the vote, confronted by a seemingly endless stream of comic postcards that poked fun at the eventuality. By 1911 some 700 women had been imprisoned for the cause; in 1913 Emily Davison became a martyr when she fell under the king's horse at the Derby and died from her injuries. Mrs Pankhurst was constantly in and out of prison, while Christmas crackers caught the mood of the moment (far left). Once war with Germany was declared, women found a new role supporting the national effort. In 1918 women over 30 years gained the right to vote and in the national election held in December were able to cast their vote for the first time. Of the 1600 parliamentary candidates, just 17 were women. Only one was elected, the Sinn Fein candidate for Dublin (she did not take the oath of allegiance to the king and thus did not attend Parliament).

Ford
THE UNIVERSAL CAR

SELLING AGENTS EVERYWHERE.

£135 COMPLETE

AT WORKS MANCHESTER

"ALL THE WORLD LOVES A 'FORD' —EVEN THE MOON BEAMS—"

Affloording a motor car became a little more possible when a range of smaller cars were produced, such as the Humberette at £125, 'so simply controlled that the veriest novice can drive it after a few minutes instruction'. The mass-produced Model T Ford had arrived in Britain in 1909; an assembly plant was established at Manchester in 1911 and the revolutionary moving production line in 1913 enabling 6000 cars to be built that year. For larger cars the idea of a turntable was available, 'a great convenience where space is limited'.

PARSIFAL AIRSHIP.
FRENCH AIRSHIP

KING'S VISIT SOUVENIR NUMBER

R·A·F
ROOSTERS and FLEDGLINGS

No. 8 R.A.F. CADET WING.

Vol. 1. No. 5.
SEPT., 1918.

The Successes of the Douglas motor cycle are proof of its Leadership. *Little from Dept. "K" KINGSWOOD, BRISTOL.*

FLYING

Vol. 5.   FEB. 5th, 1919.   *Registered as a Newspaper*   PRICE SIXPENCE

107

Contractors to the

AVRO HYDROPLANE
NIEUPORT SEA-PLANE

[4 Bouverie Street, London E.C

THE PILOTEER

October 1918

FLYING

Vol. 3. No. 59   MARCH 6th, 1918.
COMPLETE FLYING OUTFITS.

British Battle-plane squadron attacking.

British Armed Sea-plane on Patrol. R.N.A.S.

British Seaplane R.N.A.S.

FRENCH ARMOURED AEROPLANE

BATTLES IN THE AIR
by
Agnes Weston

R.F.C.

They call us THE EYES
OF THE ARMY
for we scout far and wide...

FROM ONE OF THE
R.F.C.

Fast British Scout climbing.

SPECIAL FLYING NUMBER.
THE SCOUT

FOUNDED BY
SIR ROBERT
BADEN-POWELL K.C.B.

OFFICIAL ORGAN
OF THE BOY SCOUTS

1D

No. 554.   N.V. 23, 1918.

BRITISH BIPLANES DRIVING OFF ENEMY PLANES

BRITISH AEROPLANE (VICKERS BIPLANE)
ATTACKING A TAUBE

FRANKLYN'S LAST FLIGHT
A Great R.A.F. Story.   ·   By GEORGE R. SAMWAYS.

Flying was the glamorous occupation of the time, the exploits of courageous aviators were reported in the press and illustrated in new magazines such as 'The Aero and Flight'. Boys' papers revelled in daring deeds, 'a thrilling story of adventure in the clouds'. The first British victim of aviation was claimed in 1910 when Charles Rolls (a partner in the Rolls-Royce car firm and winner of the 1,000 mile motoring trial of 1900) was killed when his aircraft crashed during a flying competition. He had recently become the first person to fly both ways across the Channel without stopping. The world's first air mail delivery was made from Hendon to Windsor in 1911. The Royal Flying Corps was established in 1912; in May 1918 it merged with the Royal Navy Air Service to form the Royal Air Force.

During the war the part played by aircraft moved from the passive reporting of troop movements and shell-fall to the more active aerial combat and harassment of ground troops. The first aircraft bombing raid on London was made in June 1917. There were many heros of the air. For Germany it was Manfred von Richthofen, the Red Baron (named after his red Fokker triplane) he shot down a record 80 allied aircraft in less than two years – but in April 1918 he was killed over the skies of France during the second battle of the Somme.

17

While the internal horn gramophone began to take over from those with an external horn, music played on a windup gramophone had become the popular sound for evening entertainment. Nevertheless, the music sheet proliferated to keep up with the latest patriotic and sentimental songs of the Great War - 'Take me back to dear old Blighty', 'Keep the Home Fires Burning' and 'Goodbye Dolly, I must leave you'. The most popular song of the war was 'It's a long, long way to Tipperary', sung by the troops of almost all the nations on both sides. The Decca portable gramophone arrived in 1914, a suitable asset for any trench.

19

THE STRANGE CASE OF M...

KINEMATOGRAPH WEEKLY SUPPLEMENT

JUNE 19, 1913.

THE ACCURATE CHECKTA...

The ORIGINAL and STANDARD Ticket Issuing Machines.

Used in all the Principal Theatres, Music Halls and Picture Palaces in London an...

Write for particulars. ACCURATE CHECKTAKER Ltd.,
and quotation. Telegram Gerrard 1915.

HIRE.

Our **5/-** services are made up of the very best films. Get in touch with us. Let us send you a suggested programme.

PICTURES AND The PICTUREGOER Vol. 7. New Series. No. 42. Week Ending SATURDAY, DEC. 5, 1914.

THE PICTURE THEATRE WEEKLY MAGAZINE.

MARY PICKFORD has appeared in the following

ESSANAY SUPER SERIAL 15 TWO-PART EPISODES

Lon Chaney as Robert Hammond
Hayward Mack as Monty Seaton

PICTURES AND The **PICTUREGOER** **1**D.

New Series. No. 39. Week Ending SATURDAY, NOV. 14, 1914. Price One Penny, Post-free, 1½d.

THE PICTURE THEATRE WEEKLY MAGAZINE.

FAMOUS PLAYERS FILMS

MARY PICKFORD,
The Famous Players' Leading Lady, and Everybody's Favourite.

THE LYRIC. ONE PENNY PROGRAMME

The Lymington and New Forest Entertainments Ltd.

high class Pictures

SECRETARY Mr. T. W. Polfrey LYMINGTON MANAGER Mr. Harry B. Winanto

ENTIRE CHANGE OF PROGRAMME EVERY MONDAY and THURSDAY

'Early Closing Day'

6ᵈ PAY HERE

PICTURE THEATRE MATINEE.

DEEDS OF DARKNESS

We're off at one o'clock — what?

FORD STERLING—The "Different" ... Who appears exclusively in "Sterling" Comic...

KING BAGGOT IN THE IMPRESSIVE IMP TWO-REEL DRAMA

GOLD IS NOT ALL

UNIVERSAL FILMS TRADE MARK

THE MONEY MANIAC

THREE IMPS EVERY WEEK IMP

"NO, NO, FAIR MAID, A CRIMSON SOUL CAN NE'ER BE WHITE"

"AS A WHITE SLAVER, YOU'RE PUNK"

HOP-HEAD'S DREAM BURLESQUE COMEDY

"AVAUNT, THOU HONEST FOOL, THE CITY'S LURE IS WITH THE SIMPLE MAID"

"THUS DO WE CROWN THEE, OH, KING OF THE DOPES"

AB **BIOGRAPH** AB

"WONDERFUL, HOW YOUR MEN HESITATE"

"THE FATHER OF YOUR CHILD HE IS THE FATHER OF ALL"

ALONG CAME A CITY CHAP BURLESQUE COMEDY

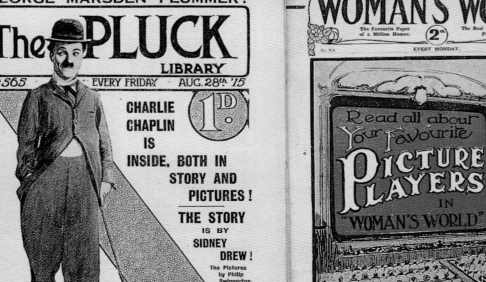

The decade saw the picture show come to the masses. Britain's purpose-built cinema had opened in 1907, and by 1912 there were some 4000 picture houses covering the country. Patronised initially by the working classes, during the war the appeal widened. In 1919 cinema magazines blossomed with Cinema Chat (free photo pin-up) and Picture Show (art plate given inside) - it meant that magazines like Woman's World had to promote their coverage of the film world.

The silent picture was accompanied by a pianist (or occasionally an orchestra) to enhance the feature film or the slapstick comedy of Charlie Chaplin, 'Fatty' Arbuckle and Ben Turpin. The darling of the screen was Mary Pickford. The pre-eminent film director was D.W. Griffiths who developed new techniques of definition, light and close-up. He made hundreds of short films such as 'Gold is not All' (arriving in Britain 1913) and the first American epic-feature film 'The Birth of a Nation' (1915).

MRS. BULL
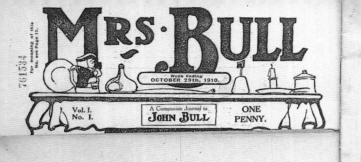

Week Ending OCTOBER 29th, 1910.

Vol. I. No. I. A Companion Journal to **JOHN BULL** ONE PENNY.

76534

No. 1 OF NEW COLOURED PAPER.

1D **The MERRY-THOUGHT & SCRAPS** 1D

Vol. I. No. I. May 7, 1910.

Fry's **PURE BREAKFAST Cocoa** ½-lb. Tin, 4½d

Makers to the Royal Households and to other Royal Courts of Europe.

SUNDAY STORIES

THIS PAPER GIVES AWAY HARRY LAUDER'S SONGS — MUSIC AND WORDS.

MY PAPER

1D

"You told me you were a single man!"

"TIRED OF HIS WIFE!"

"OUT OF REACH" — Magnificent Coloured Plate Free with this First Number

CASSELL'S FAMILY CIRCLE

Vol. 1 No. 1 March 15th, 1913

The Popular Home Weekly

1D

JOSEPH HOCKING'S NEW SERIAL

MILLION

London & Lancashire Life Office

Write for PROSPECTUS of EDUCATIONAL ENDOWMENTS and SCHOLARSHIP ANNUITIES. Chief Office: 66-67 Cornhill, E.C.

The TRAMP

AN OPEN AIR MAGAZINE

March Monthly 6d

The Girl's Own Paper & WOMAN'S MAGAZINE

Edited by FLORA KLICKMANN

SMART FICTION 1D

SERIAL STORY YOU WILL ALWAYS REMEMBER

GOLDEN STORIES

Be sure to read our amazing and thrilling serial story:—THE SHADOW ON THE PURPLE: Recollections of an Ex-Attaché. by a Peeress. A dramatic and intensely fascinating chronicle of the Secrets, Adventures, Scandals, and Intrigues of a Foreign Court.

FACT AND FICTION

A Journal of Miscellaneous Information and Entertaining Literature.

USEFUL — INTERESTING — AMUSING — INSTRUCTIVE.

Editor.

No. 1 of New Paper. Shirt Blouse Pattern and Envelope with every copy. See that you get it.

THE WOMAN'S WEEKLY

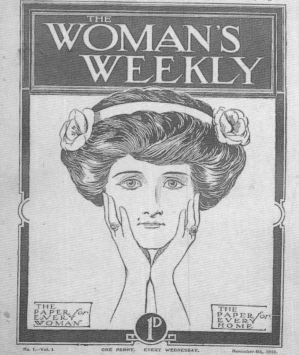

THE PAPER FOR EVERY WOMAN 1D THE PAPER for EVERY HOME

No. 1—Vol. I. ONE PENNY. EVERY WEDNESDAY. November 6th, 1911.

WOMAN'S OWN

LADIES! Here is a New Paper

MAGNIFICENT PHOTOGRAVURE FREE WITH EVERY COPY

TWENTY SUMMER DRESSES (like the one shown here) REAL GOLD BROOCHES, DAINTY CAMISOLES, LUCKY SHOE PINCUSHIONS, for Hints, Recipes, Crochet Designs & Dress Tips, Every Week.

No. 1 Vol. 1 [One Penny] May 3rd, 1913

SPORTING GOSSIP

Vol. 1 No. 3 SATURDAY, OCTOBER 4, 1913. PRICE ONE PENNY.

The New Weekly

Edited by R. A. SCOTT-JAMES.

Managing Director: A. N. PALMER.

Vol. I. No. 1. SATURDAY, MARCH 21, 1914.

WOMAN AT HOME

SEPTEMBER

SUMMER FICTION NUMBER

STORIES BY E. F. BENSON, DAVID LYALL, MARION HILL, G. VILLIERS STUART. AND OTHERS

6D net

THER AND HOME

The **HAPPY HOME**
Is it worth while?

"SUNSHINE SUE"—Charming Complete Story Within
HORNER'S WEEKLY
PRICE ONE PENNY.

WHEN THE BOYS GO MARCHING BY!

The March
Lady's Realm
1914
Woman— and Her Dog

BLIGHTY
XMAS
NUMBER 1/-

The ever-prolific magazines told stories that covered everything from romance to tragedy. The appeal was wide; "Millions" aimed to be 'the magazine for all, the largest and the best magazine ever issued for one penny'. The first issue of My Paper (1913) contained the confessions of Phyllis Dare, the musical comedy actress, and the music for Harry Lauder's 'Roamin' in the Gloamin'. Woman's Weekly was launched in 1911 ('the paper for every home').

"HOME COMPANION" IS THE FANCYWORKER'S BEST FRIEND.
HOME COMPANION 2d WAR PRICE

VICTORY FOOD! *See Striking Article Inside.*
PENNY PICTORIAL 2d WAR-TIME PRICE

Read our Great Boxing Serial
YES OR NO
The Saturday Magazine

WOMAN'S
BEAUTY AND HEALTH 2d April
THE PHYSIQUE BEAUTIFUL

"Good-bye, sonny; and take care of mummy till I come home."

A CHEERFUL PAPER FOR CHEERFUL PEOPLE
CHEERIO! 1½
FULL of FUN and FICTION
Vol. I. No. I. May 17, 1919.

ash's
& Pall Mall Magazine

Little Folks
February 1917 7d net

EVE

Exquisite SATIN PICTURES of your FAVOURITE CINEMA STARS FREE inside. 11/10/19.
No. 1
The **HOME MIRROR** 1½

Serial by Elinor Glyn.

IMPORTANT! 100 PATRIOTIC OVERALLS WILL BE OFFERED FREE NEXT WEEK.
WOMAN'S WORLD
The Favourite Paper of a Million Homes.
WAR 2d PRICE. The Real "Cheer-Up" Paper.
No. 475. EVERY MONDAY. AUGUST 24th, 1916.
"Daddy's Ship"

Vol. 1. No 1 NOVEMBER 8, 1919. PRICE 6d
PAN

No. 1. NEW STORY PAPER. No. 1.

1/2d The GIRLS' HOME 1/2d

Vol. I.—No. 1.]   ONE HALFPENNY—EVERY THURSDAY.   [March 5th, 1910.

☞ **GRAND HOLIDAY NUMBER**

1/2d Lot-o'-Fun

Vol. XIII. No. 324.   May 25th, 1912.   Price One Halfpenny.

—Sea.

"THE GIRL WITHOUT A HOME." THE FINEST STORY EVER WRITTEN. SEE PAGE 2.

Merry and Bright 1/2d

Vol. I.—No. 1.   PRICE ONE HALFPENNY.   OCTOBER 22, 1910.

CURLY KELLY, THE CHAMPION LAUGHTER PROVIDER AND SIDE-SPLITTER.

NO. 1 OF A GRAND NEW STORY-BOOK

CHEER BOYS CHEER. 1d EVERY WEDNESDAY

THE PAPER EVERY BOY CAN SHOW HIS PARENTS.

Vol. 1. No. 1.   Week ending May 25, 1912.   36 pages, One Penny.

SHUNNED BY THE VILLAGE !   Henry St. John's Great New Serial, starts in this number.

'Schoolboys' Trea

A SPLENDID NEW, LONG, COMPLETE TALE O

The **Magnet** Library

No. 217.   The Complete Story-Book

A Companion Paper
"THE GEM" LIBRARY
The Popular Thread
School-Story Book

"THE GIRL OUTCAST." THE MOST POWERFUL STORY EVER WRITTEN. SEE PAGE 2.

The **Favorite** Comic. **1/2d**

Vol. I.—No. 1.   PRICE ONE HALFPENNY.   [JANUARY 21, 1911.

No1 Vol 1 The CHAMPION January 1913 BOYS' PAPER 3d NETT

CRICKET BATS FOR READERS.   SEE PAGE 3.

1/2d Comic-Life 1d/2

No. 674.   Our Pals Have Taken to Motor-Biking.   May 20, 1911.

The BIG 1/2d. COMIC.   No. 2 OF HENDERSONS' GREAT NEW PAPER.

12 Pages of Pictures and Stories.   The Big 1d/2 Comic.   Every Wednesday

Vol. I. No. 2.   PRICE ONE HALFPENNY.   JANUARY 24, 1914.

BILL AND GET (See the

Every Monday.

FUNNYBONE THE REAL COMIC 1/2d   [Sept. 4th, 1911.

Me and My Dawg.—BEING THE 'VENTURES OF TOMMY AND STUMPY.

CHUCKLES, 1/2d. CHAMPION COLOURED COMIC.   **NEWEST AND BEST!**   CHUCKLES, 1/2d. CHAMPION COLOURED COMIC.

Chuckles 1d/2

No. 6. Vol. 1.   PRICE ONE HALFPENNY.   February 14, 1914.

SO

No.

HERE

NO. 1 OF A GRAND NEW STORY PAPER.

THE BOYS' BEST 1d STORY PAPER

No. 1.—Vol. I.   EVERY FRIDAY.—ONE PENNY.   OCTOBER 7, 1911.

No. 1. A SPLENDID TOY MODEL GIVEN FREE WITH THIS NUMBER. 1d

THE RAINBOW 1d

No. 1. Vol. I.   PRICE ONE PENNY.   February 14, 1914.

THE JOLLY ADVENTURES OF THE BRUIN BOYS.—THEIR SNOW-MAN HAS A WARM TIME.

AR

THE

AH

No. 947.]

A TOUCHING

NO. 1 OF THIS GREAT NEW STORY AND PICTURE PAPER.

The **Penny Wonder 1d** EVERY WEDNESDAY

No. 1.   EVERY WEDNESDAY.   [FEBRUARY 10, 1912.

The Biggest, Best, and Brightest.   It will Astound You.

The **Dreadnought 1d**

Vol. I.—No. 1.   EVERY FRIDAY.   [March 9, 1912.

☞ **Special War Issue**

The **Boys' Journ**

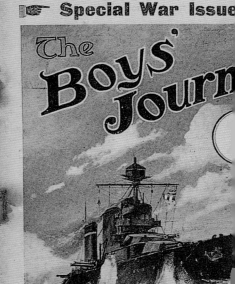

BRIGHT, BREEZY, BRACING!

Puck 1^D

EVERY THURSDAY. ONE PENNY.   SEPTEMBER 12, 1914.

No. 1 of Henderson's Great New Paper for Everyone.

12 Pages of Stories and Comic Pictures
Sparks
A Bright Paper of Stories and Sparkling Fun for Everyone.
1D/2 EVERY TUESDAY.
Vol. 1. No. 1.   PRICE ONE HALFPENNY.   MARCH 21, 1914.

The CHILDREN'S NEWSPAPER
The Story of the World Today for the Men and Women of Tomorrow
Number One   EDITED BY ARTHUR MEE   March 21, 1919.
THE CHILDREN'S LEAGUE OF NATIONS
REMARKABLE AIRSHIP DISCOVERY | What the Conference Has Forgotten | THE WAR-HORSE COMES HOME
WORLD'S AIRWAYS SAFE | The League of Nations has been born in Paris. It came into being on February 14, and there are those who believe its creation to be the greatest event in the history of the world.

ALL PROFITS TO THE BRITISH RED CROSS SOCIETY.   LOVELY COLOURED PLATE GIVEN AWAY!

Our Girls 1^d
No. 1.   PUBLISHED EVERY WEDNESDAY.   [March 6th, 1915.

No. 1 of a Great New Paper!   Photo Plate of Joe Beckett!

The Boys' REALM 1^D OF SPORT AND ADVENTURE
No. 1. Vol. I. (New Series).   April 5th, 1919.

No. 1 OF A GREAT NEW COMIC PAPER.   OUT TO-DAY.

ONE HALF PENNY ENOUGH TO MAKE A CAT LAUGH
The Halfpenny Wonder. 1^D/2
Vol. I.—No. 1.   EVERY TUESDAY.   [Week ending March 28, 1914.

No. 1.   FIRST NUMBER OF A WONDERFUL NEW PAPER.

Merry Moments 1^D/2
No. 1. Vol. I.   EVERY MONDAY.   APRIL 12, 1919.
THE ADVENTURES OF THE HAPPY TWINS AND PROFESSOR CRAZY KLEW THE DUD DETECTIVE

ING about "The Butterfly," ½d., pleases everyone, so YOU will find it will therefore please LIKE. Get a copy and see. You will find the pictures are really funny, and the stories just the sort you like.

The Firefly 1^D/2
PRICE ONE HALFPENNY.   [August 14, 1915.

NO. 1 OF THE GREAT NEW BOY'S PAPER

The BOY'S WEEKLY 1^D
A Bright Up-to-Date Paper for British Boys.
Vol. I. No. 1.   (EVERY TUESDAY.)   [MAY 3, 1919.

CHRISTMAS COMPANION!

RLS' FRIEND 1^D
ory Paper for Readers of all Ages.
ONE PENNY-EVERY TUESDAY.   [December 29th, 1917.

BEAUTIFUL COLOURED MODEL OF THE FAIRIES' CASTLE GIVEN FREE WITH THIS COPY.

The SUNDAY FAIRY 2^D
A CHARMING NEW WEEKLY PAPER FOR BOYS AND GIRLS TO READ ON SUNDAYS.

GLAND, HOME, AND BEAUTY!

EN TOMMY COMES HOME

WHEN THE GERMANS CAME TO ENGLAND!

THE 1^D PLUCK LIBRARY
EVERY FRIDAY   The Patriotic Weekly

With Presentation Plate in Colours "OFF TO THE GOLDEN WEST"

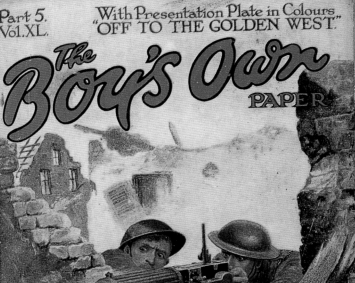
Part 5. Vol. XL.
The BOY'S Own PAPER
MARCH, 1918.
London: 4, BOUVERIE STREET, E.C. 4   9^D NET.
ALL RIGHTS RESERVED
All About Machine Guns

GREAT NEW SCHOOL STORY PAPER!

The Greyfriars Herald 1^D/2
No. 1. (New Series)   November 1, 1919.
NEW LONG SCHOOL STORY BY OWEN CONQUEST
MANY GRAND TUCK HAMPERS GIVEN AWAY!

The Boy Scout movement had been established in 1907 by Robert Baden-Powell, who then set up the Girl Guides with his sister Agnes in 1910 (their own paper came in 1914) and for his son Peter the Cub Scouts in 1914 (Wolf Cubs in 1916). With the patronage of George V the popularity of the scouts increased. Numerous board games were published; many individual Scout troops produced their own, often rudimentary, magazines.

As the box lids portrayed, many games were intended for the participation of the whole family, whether Blow-Football or Slip-Bak (where players had to pull a marble over obstacles). Another game was Hustlemee ('getting obstacles through the small rings is great fun'), promoted as being suitable for large or small parties of adults. The race game Atlantic Record reflected the prowess of ocean ships now competing for speed (in 1914 the White Star liner Britannic was the world's largest ship). Meccano had started its own magazine (just four pages) in 1916 'to help Meccano boys to have more fun than other boys'.

The hero of the hour was Kitchener who was transformed into a character doll for more well-to-do children. With the outbreak of war, patriotic games began to fill the toy shops and appear in the mail order Army & Navy catalogue. Money boxes ranged from the juvenile savings bank 'tank' to the Kaiser's piggy bank (top shelf, right). Adventure books now joined battle with stories from Tripoli and Constantinople to submarine warfare and life 'With Haig on the Somme'. The prolific story writer, Percy F. Westerman, was in his element.

Games manufacturers were quick to create topical war-related manoeuvres. The race to Berlin was on — as above in The Great European War Game (as the conflict spread to other theatres of war, it became known as the Great War). The optimistic 'Allies Invasion of Berlin' or the 'Air Raid on Berlin' never in reality took place, whereas the threat of submarines was real enough prompting such games as 'Running the Blockade' and 'Running the Gauntlet'.

Puzzles were particularly popular at this time and plenty of patriotic versions were provided. Jigsaws could be simply cut from the allies' flags ('See Daddie! We have kept the flag flying while you have been away') or could be an exceedingly difficult battle (see far right hand corner). The Mammoth picture puzzle box lid depicts a wounded soldier as the focus of attention. The puzzle 'Germany Cut to Bits' was no more than an ordinary dissected map. In January 1916 conscription was introduced for single men which inspired the game Konskripto (above). The objective of the glazed puzzles (above top) was to roll a silver ball round the course avoiding the holes. 'All British' products were now a prerequisite: many toys and games had been made in Germany prior to the war.

A NEW GUARD AGAINST ALL DISORDERS,

Keeps up
The System

THE HEALTH DRINK

NATURE'S FRUIT SALINE.

EUSALINE

MAY BE I DO LOOK BLACK
BUT I AINT NO SLACKER.
I BET THE SHELLS I'VE MADE
WILL MAKE THOSE HUNS LOOK BLACKER

NOTICE
NIGHT SHIFTS
MUST RESUME
THEIR DUTIES
PROMPTLY
AT
8 O'CLOCK

I hate working in a night shift!

NOTICE
ALL WORKERS
ON
MUNITIONS
WILL WORK IN
SHIFTS

"Well, I want to do my bit, but
I draw the line at that !!"

THE PEEK-A-BOOS
IN WAR TIME

OUR GIRLS
IN WARTIME

RHYMES BY
HAMPDEN GORDON

PICTURES BY
JOYCE DENNYS

AUTHORS OF OUR HOSPITAL A B C

LONDON JOHN LANE THE BODLEY HEAD
NEW YORK JOHN LANE COMPANY

TO NEWSAGENTS: The Government are stopping returns from May 1st. Get the
See that the customer does so before leaving your shop.

THE Family Journal
INSTRUCTIVE AND ENTERTAINING.
No. 417. Volume XVII. April 28th, 1917.

Our Popular
"I'LL TELL
YOU" BOOK

PART X
"SMAR
STOCK
GIVEN AWA
THIS ISSU

NATIONAL SERVICE

While our men FIGHT
Our women must WORK

Women are wanted!
They are wanted URGENTLY!
They are wanted AT ONCE!

Volunteer for NATIONAL SERVICE To-Day!

Fry's PURE BREAKFAST Cocoa   A LIQUID FOOD WITH SOLID VALUE.   Makers to H.M. the King

HOME COMPANION   2D. WAR PRIC

My Experiences
by One of
London's Policewomen
begins inside

No. 1-129.   EVERY MONDAY.   August 3rd, 1918.

NEWSAGENTS.   ALL YOUR CUSTOMERS will want the beautiful Picture
Portrait of Pearl White being given in next week's "Woman's
World." Please don't disappoint any of them.

WOMAN'S WORLD
The Favourite Paper of a Million Homes.   WAR 2D. PRICE.   The Best Cheer-Up Paper.

No. 168.   EVERY MONDAY.   NOVEMBER 25th, 1916.

"D.r Sal"

Welfare Superintendent

"D.r SAL" is the pretty heroine of a series of Splendid
SHORT STORIES starting inside.

NEXT WEEK'S ISSUE will contain a beautiful
PICTURE-PORTRAIT OF PEARL WHITE
the lovely Film actress.
Make sure of it by ordering your copies to-day.

THE GIRLS WENT O
AND BOYS WENT

Women in War Time
Postwoman

What nice bold
handwriting!

Women in War Time
Police woman

Pass along please!

Women in War Time
Chauffeur

Coming for
a spin?

Women in War Time
Firewoman

I'm ready!

Women found a new freedom
as they increasingly took over
the jobs of men who left to
fight at the front. They became
railway guards, postwomen,
policewomen, fire fighters,
chauffeurs and so on. Many
women were needed in
industry particulary in the
munitions factories, others helped on the
farms. Nurses were in great demand at
home and abroad. By the end of 1915 it
was said that women factory workers
were twice as good as men.

34

FORWARD!
Forward to Victory
ENLIST NOW

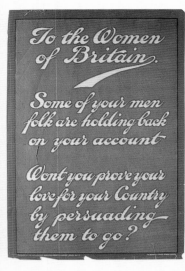

To the Women of Britain.

Some of your men folk are holding back on your account

Won't you prove your love for your Country by persuading them to go?

YOUR COUNTRY'S CALL

Isn't this worth fighting for?
ENLIST NOW

TO THE WOMEN OF BRITAIN.

1. You have read what the Germans have done in Belgium. Have you thought what they would do if they invaded this Country?

2. Do you realise that the safety of your home and children depends on our getting more men NOW?

3. Do you realise that the one word "GO" from you may send another man to fight for our King and Country?

4. When the War is over and someone asks your husband or your son what he did in the great War, is he to hang his head because you would not let him go?

WON'T YOU HELP AND SEND A MAN TO JOIN THE ARMY TO-DAY?

THERE'S ROOM FOR YOU
ENLIST TO-DAY

What in the end will settle this war?
TRAINED MEN
It is YOUR DUTY to become one

JOIN THE ROYAL MARINES
Help to man the guns of the Fleet

APPLY TO

IS YOUR HOME WORTH FIGHTING FOR?

IT WILL BE TOO LATE TO FIGHT WHEN THE ENEMY IS AT YOUR DOOR
SO JOIN TO-DAY

THE EMPIRE NEEDS MEN!

THE OVERSEAS STATES

All answer the call.
Helped by the YOUNG LIONS
The OLD LION defies his Foes
ENLIST NOW.

LINE UP, BOYS!

ENLIST TO-DAY.

Come into the ranks and fight for your King and Country—Don't stay in the crowd and stare

YOU ARE WANTED AT THE FRONT
ENLIST TO-DAY

"A Happy New Year to our Gallant Soldiers!

VICTORY
1915

You can make it certain if you
JOIN NOW

G.R.
YOUR KING & COUNTRY NEED YOU
A CALL TO ARMS

An addition of 100,000 men to His Majesty's Regular Army is immediately necessary in the present grave National Emergency.

LORD KITCHENER is confident that this appeal will be at once responded to by all those who have the safety of our Empire at heart.

TERMS OF SERVICE

General Service for the period of the war only. Age on Enlistment, between 19 and 30. Height, 5 ft. 3 in. and upwards. Chest, 34 in. at least. Medically fit.

Married Men or Widowers with Children will be accepted, and will draw Separation Allowance under Army conditions.

MEN ENLISTING FOR THE DURATION OF THE WAR will be discharged with all convenient speed, if they so desire, the moment the war is over.

HOW TO JOIN

Men wishing to join should apply at any Military Barrack or at any Recruiting Office the addresses of the latter can be obtained from Post Offices or Labour Exchanges.

GOD SAVE THE KING

THE VETERAN'S FAREWELL.

"Good Bye, my lad. I only wish I were young enough to go with you!"

ENLIST NOW!

WHICH

OUGHT YOU TO WEAR?

We're both needed to serve the Guns!

FILL UP THE RANKS!
PILE UP THE MUNITIONS!

STEP INTO YOUR PLACE

WOMEN OF BRITAIN SAY— "GO!"

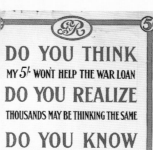

DO YOU THINK
MY 5/- WON'T HELP THE WAR LOAN

DO YOU REALIZE
THOUSANDS MAY BE THINKING THE SAME

DO YOU KNOW
IF EACH OF US SAVED 5/- A WEEK
WE SHOULD SAVE NEARLY
£600,000,000 A YEAR

INVEST YOUR 5/- TO-DAY

APPLY AT THE NEAREST POST OFFICE

WAR LOAN

LEND YOUR SAVINGS
TO THE NATION
TO-DAY

Apply for particulars at the nearest Post Office

APPEAL TO WOMEN

Make every
Penny do the
work of Two

Put your Savings
in the
WAR LOAN

You can help
to win the War
with

5/-

A SAFE AND PATRIOTIC
INVESTMENT

Apply at the nearest POST OFFICE

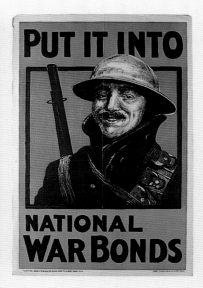

PUT IT INTO

NATIONAL
WAR BONDS

WAR LOAN

"The man, be he rich
or poor, is little
to be envied who
at this supreme
moment fails to
bring forward his
savings for the
security of his
country."

THE CHANCELLOR OF THE EXCHEQUER

Are you saving for the Children?

Save for their Education and Give
them a Start in Life
BUY
WAR SAVINGS
CERTIFICATES

THE BRITISH
SOVEREIGN
WILL WIN

INVEST
IN THE
WAR LOAN
TO-DAY

ASK FOR DETAILS AT NEAREST POST OFFICE

NOW

BACK THE BAYONETS
WITH YOUR
WAR SAVINGS
CERTIFICATES

YOU
buy War Bonds

We
do the rest.!

Write a Cheque
TO DAY
for

NATIONAL
WAR BONDS

You have in
your pocket
SILVER BULLETS
that will stop
the Germans

Lend them to
your Country
by
Investing in the
WAR LOAN
TO-DAY

BACK THEM UP

MY DUTY

INVEST IN THE
WAR LOAN

HELP YOUR COUNTRY

Invest
5/-
To-day
in the
WAR LOAN

Apply at nearest Post Office.

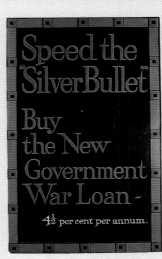

Speed the
"Silver Bullet"

Buy
the New
Government
War Loan -
4½ per cent per annum.

WAR SAVINGS
CERTIFICATES

£1 for 15/6

BUY
NATIONAL
WAR BONDS
REGULARLY
WEEK BY WEEK

The poster was an essential part of communication, to encourage men to enlist, by appealing to their patriotic duty, or to their women who were asked to persuade their men folk to go. Men were also asked to think how they would answer the question, 'Daddy, what did you do in the Great War?' (see p.60). War loans were also urgently needed as the costs escalated. In November 1914 £350m was required- the war was costing £1m a day, doubling within six months. In May 1916 the total war credit had reached £2,382m. By January 1917 the cost had risen to a staggering £5.7m a day.

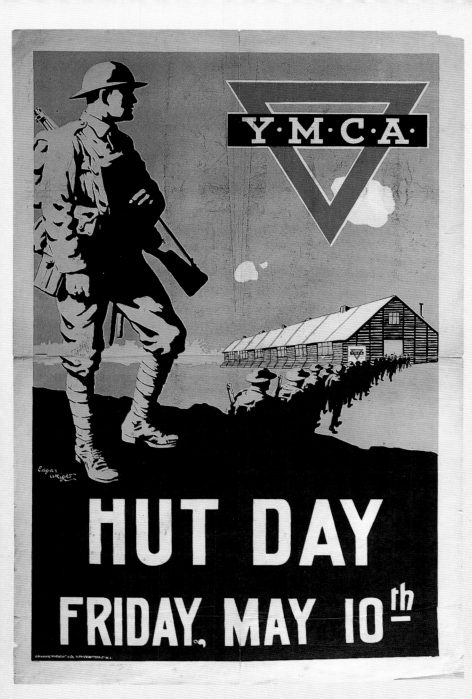

Y·M·C·A

HUT DAY
FRIDAY, MAY 10th

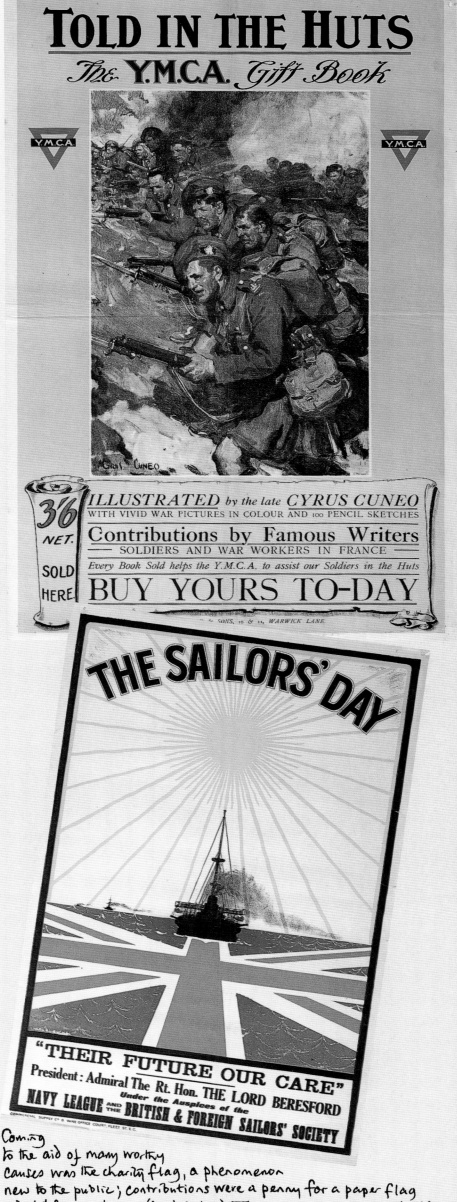

TOLD IN THE HUTS
The Y.M.C.A. *Gift Book*

Y.M.C.A.   Y.M.C.A.

3/6 NET. SOLD HERE!

ILLUSTRATED *by the late* CYRUS CUNEO
WITH VIVID WAR PICTURES IN COLOUR AND 100 PENCIL SKETCHES

Contributions by Famous Writers
SOLDIERS AND WAR WORKERS IN FRANCE

Every Book Sold helps the Y.M.C.A. to assist our Soldiers in the Huts

BUY YOURS TO-DAY

— SONS, 10 & 11, WARWICK LANE.

THE SAILORS' DAY

"THEIR FUTURE OUR CARE"
President: Admiral The Rt. Hon. THE LORD BERESFORD
Under *the* Auspices *of the*
NAVY LEAGUE *AND THE* BRITISH & FOREIGN SAILORS' SOCIETY

BLUE CROSS FUND
HELP THE WOUNDED
HORSES AT THE WAR

"OUR DUMB FRIENDS' LEAGUE"
A SOCIETY FOR THE ENCOURAGEMENT OF KINDNESS TO ANIMALS

DONATIONS IMMEDIATELY TO
ARTHUR J. COKE, Secretary.
58, VICTORIA STREET, LONDON, S.W.

Coming
to the aid of many worthy
causes was the charity flag, a phenomenon
new to the public; contributions were a penny for a paper flag
and 6d for a silk one (see left top). There were over 10,000 charities
during the war years, catering for every need (Birmingham cripples
to the YMCA Hut fund where soldiers could rest). However there were
some disreputable charities. Ingenious ways to raise funds included
the sale of patriotic perfumed sachets and souvenir stamps.
The Belgium Relief fund competition (Sept. 1914) involved painting 26 adverts. **39**

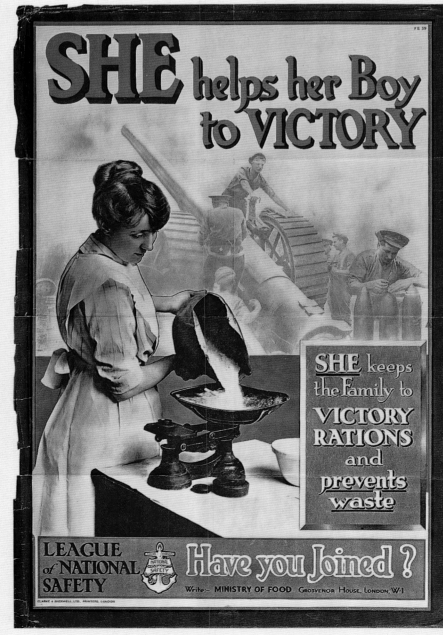

Posters
shout their message.
The cost of bread reached record levels in
1916, and in May 1917 the King urged everyone to eat less
bread. Along with potatoes and fresh eggs, meat was also in
short supply; restaurants could not serve meat one day a week
by the end of 1916 (increased to two days in Jan 1918). General
rationing was announced in June 1918 and the issue of ration books.
The publications of Arthur Mee during 1917-18 highlighted the
amount of grain and sugar used to create alcohol (£300m a yr.).

40

THE FIDDLERS

ARTHUR MEE

HOW LONG WILL YOU GO ON FIDDLING? TILL WE STARVE?

HOUSEHOLD RYE BREAD.

1 lb. rye flour.   1 teaspoonful sugar.
½ lb. ground rice.   1 teaspoonful salt.

WAR FLOURS

AS AN ENTIRE SUBSTITUTE FOR
WHITE FLOUR

MINISTRY OF FOOD.

RATIONING ORDER, 1918.

Instructions for the use of the New Ration Card.

MINISTRY OF FOOD. Serial No. L.O. 1 No. 235839

NATIONAL RATION BOOK (B).

INSTRUCTIONS.
[Read carefully.]

MINISTRY OF FOOD. Serial No. Ch 66 No. 0256

CHILD'S RATION BOOK (A).

INSTRUCTIONS.
[Read carefully.]

FOOD CARD.
London and Home Counties.

RATION CARD

ISSUED TO ALL REGISTERED CUSTOMERS OF

J. SAINSBURY

BUTTER RATION 2 OUNCES PER WEEK.

| 2 | 3 | 4 | 5 | 6 | 7 | 8 | 9 |
| 10 | 11 | 12 | 13 | 14 | 15 | 16 | 17 | 18 |

SUGAR RATION 12 OUNCES WEEKLY.

| 2 | 3 | 4 | 5 | 6 | 7 | 8 | 9 |
| 10 | 11 | 12 | 13 | 14 | 15 | 16 | 17 | 18 |

RATIONING SCHEME

MINISTRY OF FOOD. R 2.
RATIONING ORDER, 1918.

PURCHASER'S SHOPPING CARD.

MEAT.

Meat Ration Card

FORTHCOMING GOVERNMENT SUGAR RATIONS.
To CLARKSON'S, Grocers & Provision Dealers.

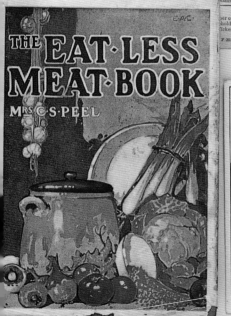

THE EAT·LESS MEAT·BOOK

MRS C. S. PEEL

S·O·S

The Facts about the Great Food Scandal
told in a few minutes for a working man

By ARTHUR MEE

Completing 300,000

1d Delivered anywhere: 50, 4/-; 100, 7/-; 250, 15/- **1d**
One Million Copies
of Arthur Mee's Books for the Prohibition Crusade
Published by MORGAN & SCOTT, Paternoster Buildings, E.C. 4

Shall we be Starved into Peace?

A 4lb Loaf of War Time Bread
(Eat half a pound a day)
Some Margarine, and Butter Beans.
A'int Bad Grub anyway!

FOOD in WAR TIME

PUBLISHED BY
G. BELL & SONS, LIMITED,
YORK HOUSE, PORTUGAL STREET, LONDON, W.C.

THREEPENCE NET

85th THOUSAND
REVISED AND ENLARGED
to 64 PAGES

EAT LESS BREAD

THREE SLICES AMONG FOUR OF US
THANK GOODNESS THERE'S NO MORE OF US.

No Cakes, no Jam, no Sugar, no nuffin!

"Come again and bring your sugar!"

Will you call for your joint later, mum?
No; you might just enclose it in an envelope and post it!

CAN'T HELP IT—
I'VE USED ALL ME MEAT COUPONS.

DON'T EAT
OR
DRINK
MORE THAN IS
NECESSARY TO
YOUR
HEALTH
AND
EFFICIENCY

"War-FARE."

I SAY WAITER! WOULD YOU MIND CLOSING THAT DOOR—I DON'T WANT MY MEAT RATION BLOWN AWAY

The Voice From Far Away

When our beloved Motherland going to believe the Facts?
Can you not find space to express the opinion of an Englishman who loves England as his life, and a hurt every time he has to listen to the facts of wasted food and degraded manhood and wasted efficiency, just because we won't tackle the strangling liquor traffic as we do the Huns?
— Wilfred Grenfell of Labrador to The Times.

Did you hear this thrilling voice from Grenfell of Labrador? Do you know the facts that have reached him so far away? Listen!

870,000 loaves are destroyed every day in this famine-threatened land

By Submarines 120,000
By Breweries 750,000

We must have ships, and still more ships.
Stopping Drink will save 1,000,000 tons

We must save food, and still more food.
Stopping Drink will save one day's bread a week for all

We must have men, and still more men.
Stopping Drink will give us 10 to 30% more man-power

We must save money, and still more money.
Stopping Drink will save £300,000,000 a year

The appalling facts that have stirred Dr. Grenfell so far away are all in

Arthur Mee's New Book
THE PARASITE 6d.

In Honour Bound
WE ADOPT
THE NATIONAL SCALE
OF
Voluntary Rations

M.F. 9.

How to Save Money in War Time

ONE SHILLINGSWORTH OF
FOOD FOR TENPENCE.

THE NATIONAL
FOOD ECONOMY LEAGUE
HANDBOOK
FOR HOUSEWIVES

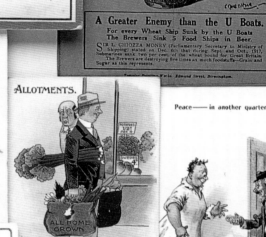

A Greater Enemy than the U Boats.
For every Wheat Ship Sunk by the U Boats
The Brewers Sink 5 Food Ships in Beer.
SIR L. CHIOZZA MONEY (Parliamentary Secretary to Ministry of Shipping) stated on Dec. 8th that during Sept. and Oct., 1917, Submarines sank two per cent. of the wheat bound for Great Britain. The Brewers are destroying five times as much foodstuffs—Grain and Sugar, as this represents.

"Thank God for a Garden!"

ALLOTMENTS.

NOW OUR ALLOTMENTS ARE IN VOGUE,
WE'LL GIVE THREE HEARTY CHEERS,
FOR THE STUFF IS GOOD AND ALL HOME GROWN,
AND WE BEAT THE PROFITEERS.

Peace—in another quarter!

Here's one or two valuables to show I don't forget you in these hard times!

RECIPES THAT HELP YOU TO RATION.
HOME COOKERY
January, 1918.
2D

Chief Contents

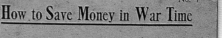

YOU PRICELESS OLD THING!!

IF HE KEEPS ON MAKING MONEY AT THIS RATE, HE'LL SOON BE TOO PROUD TO SPEAK TO HIS POOR FATHER.

6d

EGGS
5/6
PER DOZ

I HEAR YOU ARE DOING WELL AT SHELL MAKING.

"Dear Juliet,—We are showing the Germans now which side their bread's buttered!..."

Buttered, is it! They're lucky—it's margarined with us!

RISEN FROM THE RANKS.

MARGARINE

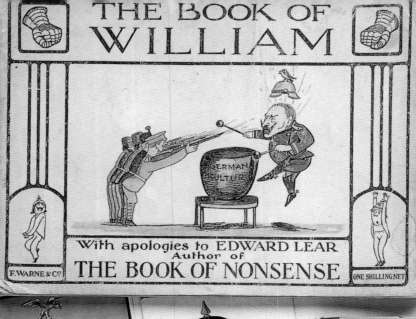

THE BOOK OF WILLIAM

With apologies to EDWARD LEAR
Author of
THE BOOK OF NONSENSE

F. WARNE & C°
ONE SHILLING NET

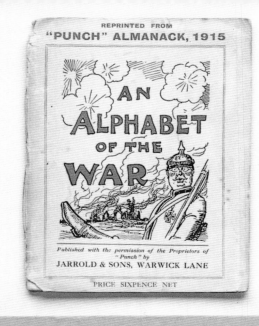

REPRINTED FROM
"PUNCH" ALMANACK, 1915

AN
ALPHABET
OF THE
WAR

Published with the permission of the Proprietors of
"Punch" by
JARROLD & SONS, WARWICK LANE

PRICE SIXPENCE NET

MALICE
IN
KULTURLAND

BY HORACE WYATT
ILLUSTRATIONS BY TELL

PUBLISHED BY
"THE CAR ILLUSTRATED"
62. Pall Mall. London. S.W.

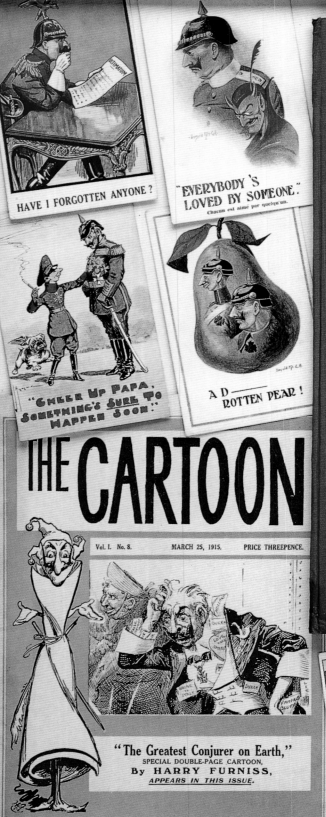

HAVE I FORGOTTEN ANYONE?

"EVERYBODY'S LOVED BY SOMEONE."
Chacun est aimé par quelqu'un.

"CHEER UP PAPA, SOMETHING'S SURE TO HAPPEN SOON."

A D—ROTTEN PEAR!

THE CARTOON

Vol. I. No. 8.   MARCH 25, 1915.   PRICE THREEPENCE.

"The Greatest Conjurer on Earth,"
SPECIAL DOUBLE-PAGE CARTOON,
By HARRY FURNISS,
APPEARS IN THIS ISSUE.

SOME
'FRIGHTFUL'
WAR PICTURES

KULTUR KULTUR
DIE WACHT AM RHEIN
BERNHARDI AM TAG
NIETZSCHE DEUTSCHLAND ÜBE
GOTT STRAFE ENGLAND
LTUR KULTUR TREITSCHKE
R KULTUR KULTUR AM TAG

BY
W·HEATH·ROBINSON

THE KAISER'S LAST LINE OF DEFENC

CENSORED CENSORED

WHAT DOES LITTLE BIRDIE SAY
IN HIS NEST AT BREAK OF DAY?

GOAL!

IN THE BEGINING
ALL THE TROUBLE
WAS CAUSED BY
AN APPLE

NOW IT'S A PAIR!

HIS FINAL RETREAT.

CANADA INDIA JAPAN RUSSIA
BRITAIN
FRANCE
BELGIUM

TO BERLIN

IT NEVER RAINS BUT IT POURS

THE KAISER'S KALENDAR FOR 1915.
OR THE DIZZY DREAM OF DEMENTED WILLIE

Price:
ONE
PENNY

BY
S. STRUBE
& W.F. BLOOD.

"'HUN'-EASY LIES THE HEAD—"

SWOLLEN-HEADED WILLIAM
(AFTER THE GERMAN!)

VERSES ADAPTED BY
E. V. LUCAS

DRAWINGS ADAPTED BY
GEO. MORROW

METHUEN & CO., LTD., 36 Essex Street, Strand, London, W.C.

ONE SHILLING NET

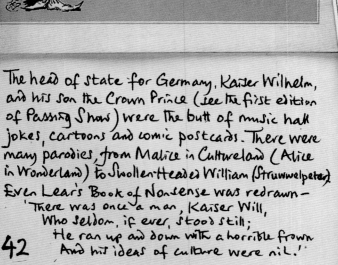

The head of state for Germany, Kaiser Wilhelm,
and his son the Crown Prince (see the first edition
of Passing Show) were the butt of music hall
jokes, cartoons and comic postcards. There were
many parodies, from Malice in Kultureland (Alice
in Wonderland) to Swollen-Headed William (Struwwelpeter).
Even Lear's Book of Nonsense was redrawn—
'There was once a man, Kaiser Will,
Who seldom, if ever, stood still;
He ran up and down with a horrible frown
And his ideas of culture were nil.'

42

A Thing of Booty

FALL IN AND FOLLOW ME.

"Bill wanted the earth—
he'll get it, too!"

YES, BUT WE DON'T;
SO IT ISN'T.

WANTED
FOR
MURDER

WILLIAM HOHENZOLLERN & CO.,
WHOLESALE BUTCHERS.

WILHELM
the RUTHLESS

(Wilhelm der Rücksichtslose)

3/6
NETT.

NOBODY LOVES ME.

"NOBODY LOVES ME"

"LOR! AND HERE I TRIED FOR THIRTY YEARS, AND CAN'T GET ONE!"

"Ah! P'raps that'll stop some of them there Gas Attacks!"

"THERE! GERTIE! HOW CAN WE GIRLS HOPE TO GET HUSBANDS WHEN THE BOYS ARE ALL GETTING ENGAGED TO THESE FOREIGN HUSSIES!"

"DEAR LORD, IF YOU'RE STILL MAKING LITTLE BOYS CAN'T I BE CHANGED INTO ONE — NOW?"

Mon Dieu, si vous — encore des petits garçons, ne pourriez-vous —

"WELL, I DON'T SUPPOSE IT HURT 'IM ANY MORE THAN SOME OF THE WOUNDS THAT OUR POOR FELLERS GET!!"

"but I'd be satisfied with far less, so come & join me"

A YOUNG RECRUIT.

"NOW IS NO TIME TO HESITATE."

"OH, LORD, TAKE CARE OF KITCHENER, FOR IF ANYTHING SHOULD HAPPEN TO HIM, WE'D HAVE NOBODY TO LOOK AFTER US BUT THE DAILY MAIL."

A SPY!

SO'S MINE!

Poor man! Have you been wounded?
No!. I've been having a tooth out!

always was unlucky!

CHEER UP, WE AIN'T THE FIRST THAT'S HAD TO DO IT.

Appeal dismissed—to be called up at once!

"I CAN'T LOVE A FELLER WHAT HASN'T DIED FOR HIS COUNTRY!"

"POOR MAN! AND HAVE YOU BEEN WOUNDED AT THE FRONT?"
"NO, MA'AM — AT THE BACK!"

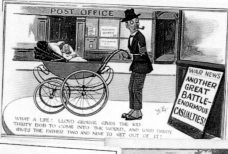

"WHAT A LIFE! LLOYD GEORGE GIVES THE KID THIRTY BOB TO COME INTO THE WORLD, AND LORD DERBY GIVES THE FATHER TWO AND NINE TO GET OUT OF IT!"

Too Old at Fifty, not a bit!
We'll let 'em see we've got some Go
For the British Oak as everyone kn—
The Longer it lives the Tougher it Gr—

This isn't "Somewhere in France" —
it's "Anywhere in England"

SOMEWHERE IN FRANCE — I MUSTN'T SAY ANYTHING MORE ABOUT IT!

"MY FATHER'S IN THE 'AIR SERVICE! WHAT, IN THE ROYAL AIR FORCE? NO 'AIR DRESSER."

WAS FIT WHEN I JOINED THE ARMY, BUT NOW MY HEART IS AFFECTED!

HE LOOKED SMARTER IN KHAKI — BUT I LOVE HIM BEST IN THIS!

I SEE YOU'RE BACK FROM THE FRONT!

Here, I say— I'm a conscientious objector!

I wish this war was over—
I've never been able to keep warm since they called him up

"YES MUM! THE BULLET JUST MISSED ME 'EART. BUT YOUR HEART ISN'T DOWN THERE. IT WAS THEN MUM."

They hopped me here
They hopped me there
Until I felt quite balmy
They felt my pulse an' told me to 'Cough!'
An' passed me into the Army.

WHEN YOU COME HOME ON LEAVE.

Sentry duty here is far from unpleasant.

GLAD YOU'RE ALL RIGHT, NOW YOU'VE ALL LEFT! YOU'LL DO ALL WRONG, IF YOU DON'T ALL WRITE!

"Have you ever had a dream like this?"

"Young man, I hope you came by all those things honestly?"

"The Cold Shoulder"
The chap who did not enlist, and now wishes that he had.

"Why aren't you at the Front, my man?"
"'Cos there ain't no milk that end, Miss!!"

I'll bet her husband's been called up!

"You see I have joined at last"
"I s'pose they're not so particular now,"

"You'll have had some narrow escapes from death."

"Rather! — I once fell out of a pram when I was a kid."

When she gives you a smile so sweet
And says you must not mind,
You know that she's hard to beat
Although she's a lot behind.

Only two gallons a week! — Why, I shift that in beer in a day, never mind a week!

THE OPTIMIST.
"IN SORRY TO HEAR SAMMY THORNE HAD YOUR ARM BLOWN OFF THAT'S NOTHING — IT MIGHT A' BEEN WORSE — I 'OUGHT"

I'm "roughing" it a bi

MERRY and BRIGHT.

WHEN THERE'S FIGHTING TO BE DONE.
TRUST THE MAN BEHIND THE GUN.

CHEER UP!
THINGS ARE NOT SO BLACK AS THEY LOOK

THERE ARE SOME
FINE OPENINGS IN
KITCHENER'S ARMY!

Here's Luck!

"FULL MARCHING ORDER"
WHAT YOUR KIT FEELS LIKE
AFTER TEN MILES!

I SHOULD LIKE TO
JOIN 'EM AT THE FRONT.

AFTER A DAY'S
MARCH
THEY FEEL AS HEAVY
AS THIS. 'PON MY SOLE!

THOUGH
YOU HAVE
SCORES
OF LETTERS
AND
LOTS OF
POSTCARDS
TOO
NONE BEARS
MORE LOVING
WISHES
THAN THIS
I SEND TO
YOU.

Are we downhearted? No! No! No!

LATEST WAR NEWS!

"THE REAR, WHICH WAS
SOMEWHAT EXPOSED,
IS NOW BEING
STRONGLY
REINFORCED!"

I've put on two stone
since I joined

← BACK TO BERLIN.

Don't be Alarmed,
the Post Office Rifles
are on guard at Cuckfield.

RALLY ROUND THE FLAGS, BOYS!

"This puts the tin hat on it!!"

The Bulldog, The French Poodle, The Russian Borzoi & the Japanese Spaniel
ARE ALL AFTER THE MAD DACHSHUND

WHAT DID YOU DO
IN THE GREAT WAR?

PUT ME DOWN YOU FOOL
YOU'LL GET THE V.C. and
I'M GETTIN' ALL THE
BULLETS IN ME PANTS.

A CERTAIN CURE FOR THE
GERMAN MEASLES.

Mix some Woolwich Powders with Tinct. of Iron or Essence
of lead, and administer in pills (or shells). Have ready a little British
Army (a little goes a long way) some Brussels Sprouts and French
Mustard. Add a little Canadian Cheese and Australian Lamb and
season with the best Indian Curry. Set it on a Kitchener and keep
stirring until quite hot.

If this does not make the Patient perspire freely, rub the best
Russian Bears' Grease on his chest and wrap in Berlin Wool.
Dr. Cannon's Prescrip.

P.S.—The patient must on no account have any
Peace-Soup until the swelling in the head
has quite disappeared.

Are we down-hearted? No! No! No!

JUST A LINE
WE'RE HOLDING
OUR OWN IN THE
TRENCHES

WELL, WHO JOLLY WELL WANTS TO GO TO CALAIS?—I DON'T.

DOWN IN OUR
BLINKING CAMP.
To the tune of "Back Home in Tennessee."

I'm so lonely, oh, so lonely,
In our Blinking Camp,
I'm like a bloomin' tramp,
Not worth a penny stamp.
Father, Mother, Sister, Brother,
All are waiting me.
I'm getting thinner, miss my dinner,
And my Sunday's tea.
CHORUS:
Down in our Blinking camp,
We're always on the ramp,
That's where we cop the cramp,
Through sleeping in the damp,
All we can hear there each day,
Is Left . . . Right . . . march away.
Sergeants calling, Lance-jacks bawling
"Get out On Parade."
We go to bed at night,
It is a glorious sight,
The earwigs on the floor,
Double-up and then Form Fours,
Then when daylight is dawning,
You can hear our Sergeant yawning
Show-a-leg there, Show-a-leg there,
Down in our Blinking Camp.

WHEN
THE WAR
STARTED.
WHEN
THE WAR
ENDS.

For gootness sake go back! Here
kom der BRITISH.

GREAT
BRITAIN

GET OUT, AND GET UNDER.

DAILY ROUTINE.
6 A.M. REVEILLE.
7 —   BREAKFAST
8·15   PARADE
9·15   20 MILE MARCH
11·15 SWEDISH DRILL
1 P.M. DINNER
2   MANCEUVRES
4   DISMISS
5   TEA
6   OUT OF BOUNDS
10   LIGHTS OUT
AND THEN
WE HAVE THE REST OF THE
DAY TO OURSELVES.

CHARGE!

The A.S.C. at Romsey Remount
Camp are Ready!

NOW ARE WE ALL HERE?
YES!!

The comic postcard reflected
the humorous side of life
on the home front and the
rigours (or not) of soldiering.
Clearly there was fun to be
had with newspaper headlines,
recruiting posters, romantic
posters and even the
wounded and bandaged soldiers. 45

At the outset of war in August 1914, there was great optimism that hostilities would be over by Christmas. Alas, it was not to be. However there was one small unofficial truce when German and British soldiers fraternised (as illustrated above in The Sphere). With patriotic Christmas cards soon on sale at home, it was not until Xmas 1916 that individual Corps and divisions created their own greetings cards, designed by a talented artist recruited from within their ranks. Silk postcards (produced by A. Benoiston & Cie, Paris) which often contained message cards (see p.1) could be purchased all along the front line. The magazine Blighty (the name given by the forces for 'home') was sent to troops free from its launch in May 1916 – the Xmas number here was the first to be sold at home to raise funds for future free publication.

FINISH JOHNNY!

GREETINGS FROM THE SALONIKA ARMY

XMAS - 1918.

BEST WISHES from the XIII CORPS

CHRISTMAS GREETINGS 1917

56th LONDON DIVISION T.F.

THE NEW YEAR WITH No.1. HEAVY ARTILLERY GROUP

YPRES - CHRISTMAS - 1917

XMAS 1917

GREETINGS FROM ROYAL ARTILLERY XIII CORPS.

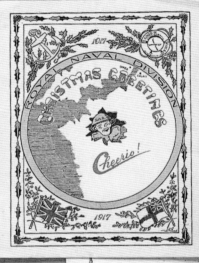

ROYAL NAVAL DIVISION XMAS GREETINGS Cheerio! 1917

CHEERIO! All's Well FRANCE CHRISTMAS 1918.

GREETINGS FROM THE 41st DIVISION CHRISTMAS 1917

From George

CHRISTMAS GREETINGS France 1918

UNITED STATES NAVAL FORCES IN EUROPE CHRISTMAS 1918

SOISSONS ARRAS YPRES

"the noble Thistle of Scotland will flourish ever amidst the Roses of FRANCE."

"CHEERIO" PELICANS XMAS 1917

GREETINGS XMAS 1918 To those at the Front To Friends at Home FRANCE LINES OF COMMUNICATION

Presentation Plate. Christmas Greeting. By The Poet Laureate.

XMAS 1917

"STILL HERE"

WITH BEST WISHES from 15TH SCOTTISH DIVISION

XMAS GREETINGS 7th Division 1916.

Ypres Neuve Chapelle Festubert Givenchy Loos The Somme

To Bring You Christmas Greetings

BLIGHTY SERVICE XMAS NUMBER.

EVERY COPY SOLD SENDS THREE TO THE TRENCHES.

GREETINGS FROM MACHINE GUN SCHOOL FRANCE. CHRISTMAS. 1916.

140th BRIGADE Christmas Greetings and a Wish for the New Year 1918

With Every Good Wish 1918 1919 For Christmas and the New Year From The 31st Division

XV ARMY CORPS

XMAS 1916

6d PICTURES AND HUMOUR FROM OUR MEN AT THE FRONT 6d

WISHING YOU ALL A HAPPY CHRISTMAS

AN ANXIOUS MOMENT

GHQ Greetings

Xmas. 1918.

Humour kept up the morale of Tommy soldier, and it was Bruce Bairnsfather's Old Bill character who became the cartoon hero of the war, reflecting the arduous conditions of life at the front – the mud, the close-shave shell fire and the monotony of bully beef and plum jam. It was this environment in which Bairnsfather made his sketches while serving with the first Warwickshire Regiment. His drawings were published in the Bystander magazine from November 1914, and later compiled in Fragments from France – the first volume sold over 250,000 copies. Appearing on jigsaws, mugs and as mascot dolls, Old Bill took to the stage in 1919 and then his own magazine Fragments was launched.

49

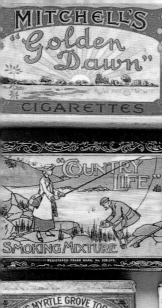

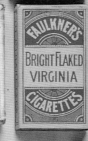

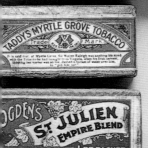

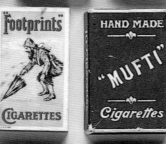

ABDULLA CIGARETTES

TURKISH, EGYPTIAN AND VIRGINIAN

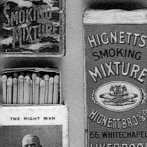

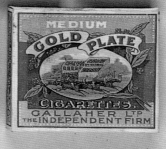

Cigarette smoking became increasingly popular during the 1910s especially with the troops; it was convenient, and by the end of the war was preferred to the more traditional pipe. The inclusion of cigarette cards was a bonus, some were shaped, like the allied soldiers and flags. By 1917 the shortage of paper prevented further production. Amongst new brands was Mufti (1915), the services term for plain clothes dress when out of uniform.

51

MOIR'S
THE SEVILLE ORANGE MARMALADE

Messrs Moirs During the War I have had many a sample of jam and marmalade by different makers but the greatest treat was a tin of Moirs Marmalade. Obviously I am not an artist but I am a bit of an epicure and I can safely say that I secured my greatest capture of the war. You may call this an unsolicited testimonial nevertheless it is one of appreciation from

Sincerel..

A Great Capture

By an idle man with a wee bit o'pencil

JOHN MOIR & SON, LTD.,
LONDON.

'Comforts for the troops' was something in which many at home could become involved, sending soap, sweets, or special Oxo boxes that contained a trench heater outfit. Chocolate was a popular gift; Rowntrees sent a tin (above right) that had a compartment with six postcards of York scenes. The British Grocers Federation sent an oval toffee tin (here with George V and Union Jack flag) 'to our fighting heroes' for Xmas 1914. Princess Mary sent a brass tin with tobacco and cigarettes (above), officers who received a pipe; for Xmas 1915 the tin contained a bullet-shaped pencil. Queen Alexandra provided cigarettes in 1914 and again in 1915. Certificates were given to schoolchildren who had contributed to the comforts.

Late News.

Important News received as this Edition was going to press will be found on the back page.

THE ECHO
AND LONDON
EVENING CHRONICLE

FIRST EDITION

NO. 1.

LONDON MONDAY MARCH 22 1915.

ONE HALFPENNY.

ANOTHER ZEPPELIN IS A WRECK!

ZEPPELIN WRECKED AT LIEGE.

Probably One of the Fleet Meant for Paris.

TO-DAY'S NEWS OF THE GREAT FIASCO

To-day the following welcome message was received in London:—
AMSTERDAM, Monday.
Persons who have arrived at Maastricht from Liege report that on Saturday a Zeppelin airship was wrecked at Liege.—Central News.

GERMAN LINER'S DASH FOR LIBERTY.

GIFT TO "ECHO" READERS.

DARING CITY FRAUD.
Forger's Application For Employment

61 BRITISH LOSSES IN THE DARDANELLES.

The Special Constable

Puzzle:—*Find the Zeppelin*

Kent Education Committee.
AIR RAIDS.

In the London Raid on the 13th June, though most of the children were in school. TWICE as many were injured among those who were NOT IN SCHOOL as among those who were.

This shows that
The School is the safest place for children during an Air Raid.

If an Air Raid should take place in your neigh—

ZEPPELIN AND ACCIDENT INSURANCE.

£10,000 FREE COMPENSATION FUND.

The Proprietors of "THE DAILY NEWS" will pay up to

£250
in the case of damage by Aerial Attack;

£25
in the case of damage by Bombardment from the Sea, or by our own Anti Aircraft Guns.

The Ocean Accident and Guarantee Corporation, Limited,

To obtain the above benefits the reader must order "The Daily News" from his newsagent and obtain from him this

Bombarding the Zepps

5 4 3 2 1

SIX

ZEPPELIN AND AEROPLANE BOMBS ON LONDON

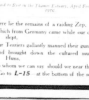

D — those Raiders.

THE FINEST SI—
I EVER SA—

LONDON BY NIGHT.

THE AIR RAI—

First bit of luck I've had for years she's going to buy one.

Na' then! things **are** getting serious, and no error.

NOTICE:
THIS PUBLIC HOUSE CLOSED OWING TO DAMAGE BY ZEPPELINS

ZEPPELIN RAIDS
RESPIRATORS AS USED AT THE FRONT
SURE SAFEGUARD AGAINST POISONOUS GAS BOMBS

Since the Zeppelins have come to Town
I always wear my best night gown,
And tie my hair with a big blue bow
In case they call on me you know.

COLMAN'S MUSTARD
COLMAN'S STARCH
COLMAN'S BLUE

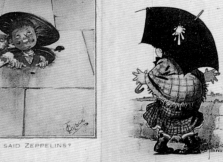

WHO SAID ZEPPELINS?

Help! Murder!
The Zepps have come!

"SHOULDN'T BE SURPRISED TO SEE A ZEPPELIN RAID TO-NIGHT!"

Poor soul! I wonder if she's been hit with a Zeppelin Bomb.

BEST PICTURES
CONTINUOUS PROGRAMME
HIS ONLY SWEETHEART
IN TWO PARTS

ZEPPELIN WIRE.
Given by H.M. War Office exclusively to the British Red Cross Society.

A NASTY JAR FOR THE BABY-KILLERS

THE EVENING PRAYER.
If the Zeppelins drop a bomb,
May I miss them every one;
But if a Zepp. doth drop a man,
I shall catch him *if* I can.
Ah-men!

You did startle me; I thought you were a Zeppelin.

SOUVENIR
*In * Loving * Memory*
OF THE
MEN, WOMEN AND CHILDREN
KILLED IN
The London Air Raid
ON WEDNESDAY, JUNE 13TH 1917,

Killed—104. Seriously injured—154. Slightly injured—269. Total—527.
The casualties include 120 children either killed or injured.

"SUFFER LITTLE CHILDREN TO COME UNTO ME, FOR OF SUCH IS THE KINGDOM OF HEAVEN."

Those tiny school babes, our little ones,
Had ceased their tasks and were listening with bated breath,
For the blotting out of the glorious sun
By the broken thunder of the German Death.

"IN THE MIDST OF LIFE, WE ARE IN DEATH."

COUNTY BOROUGH OF BURTON-UPON-TRENT.
ELECTRICITY DEPARTMENT.
ELECTRICITY SUPPLY AND AIR RAIDS.

Should information be received of the approach of enemy air-craft, the pressure at the Electricity Works will be reduced to one-half for a period of Three Minutes, then the light will be put on and off three times in quick succession, and finally out. This will be done so that the public may distinguish between a warning and an accidental failure of supply.

Power consumers should see that their motor starters are left in

One of the terrors of the war was the Zeppelin airship raid, dropping bombs over London. Although postcard humour made fun of them, they were a constant threat. The first Zeppelin was brought down in Sept 1916; souvenirs of its wire (right) were sold by the British Red Cross. Colman's devised an ingenious indicator of Zeppelin raids (above) according to weather conditions — the barometer, wind direction and strength. Since **54** 1915 blackouts had been enforced.

Printer, S. Burgess, 6, Tuck Place, Strand, London, W.

The Great War created heroes famous enough to accompany the King on tins, chocolate boxes and banners, such as the victory of Jutland souvenir with Admiral Sir John Jellicoe and Vice Admiral Beatty – although hailed as a success this naval battle inflicted heavy losses on both sides. As the new Secretary for War, Lord Kitchener received much attention; he had realised the war would be a long struggle and quickly recruited many volunteers with his poster campaign (see p. 2); in 16 months 2½ million had come to serve King and Country. In June 1916 Kitchener was drowned at sea; he was on his way to Russia when the cruiser Hampshire struck a mine and sank. Another hero of the Boer War was Field Marshall Earl Roberts, commander of overseas forces in 1914. It was Sir John French who commanded the British Expeditionary force in France, but after 16 months he was replaced by Sir Douglas Haig. The Allies were celebrated; the Belgian King and the French commander General Joffre, for instance, appeared on packs of Fry's Campaign chocolate cigarettes. BUT there were many unsung heroes, whose features were perpetuated only in family photograph albums or in glorious patriotic shrouds, framed with pride. Thousands returned home to loved ones, but nearly one million from the British Empire did not – this was the cost of war.

Union Series

"THE" **VICTORY STREAMER**

BRITISH MADE.

Germany Surrenders

Name:

Welcome Home

SPECIAL VICTORY NUMBER.   FINAL NIGHT EDITION

ROYAL EXCHANGE ASSURANCE A.D. 1720
FIRE AND ACCIDENT INSURANCES.

The Globe
AND TRAVELLER. Founded 1803.
No. 38,482. MONDAY EVENING, NOV. 11, 1918. ONE PENNY.

ROYAL
AS

LIFE
AS

VICTORY!

GERMANY SURRENDE

OUR TERMS ACCEPTED TO-DA

LAST SHOTS FIRED AT 11 A.M.

KING AND QUEEN DRIVE THROUGH LONDON T REMARKABLE SCENES.

The War is over. The last shots were fired at 11 a.m. to-day, the armistice been signed at 5 o'clock this morning.

FURNISH ON OUR SENSIBLE SYSTEM.
GRESHAM FURNISHING STORES, LTD.

The Star PEACE

No. 3842. LONDON, MONDAY, NOVEMBER 11, 1918. ONE PENNY.

THE WAR IS OVER

(Official.)

| TERMS PRINTED IN BERLIN. | ROYAL FAMILY ON BALCONY. |

Commons to be Told This Afternoon.

"THE LEFT BANK OF THE RHINE."

ARMISTICE SIGNED AT 5 A.M. TO-DAY.

Hostilities Cease on All Fronts Six Hours Later.

THE NEWS.

VICTORY !

Zonophone Record
No. 1896 2/6

THE FINEST DESCRIPTIVE RECORD EVER ISSUED

Part I. Arrival of Troops in London

Part II. The Royal Review

PEACE

I WAS NEARLY SQUEEZED DEATH IN THE CROWD

PEACE

CEASE FIRE! — BUT DON'T PUT THESE 'ARMS

Written M. STUART N

PEACE

JUST A HAPPY GREETING ON A P.C.

PEACE

THE WAY TO GIVE THANKS IS ON YOUR KNEES!

Colman's Mustard

VICTORY

GRAND PEACE RECORD

No 1896 2/6

COME INSIDE AND HEAR IT

The guns fell silent in Europe on the 11th hour of the 11th day of the 11th month of 1918. The armistice had been signed earlier that day in a railway carriage. In Britain there was jubilation after four and a half years of war. The Treaty of Versailles set out the conditions of peace in 200 pages of text; it was signed in June 1919. By the time of the victory parades held in July, there were plenty of celebration mugs, bunting and gramophone records available. As a monument to the fallen, the Cenotaph war memorial in Whitehall was designed by Sir Edward Lutyens and unveiled in July 1919 (see page 3).

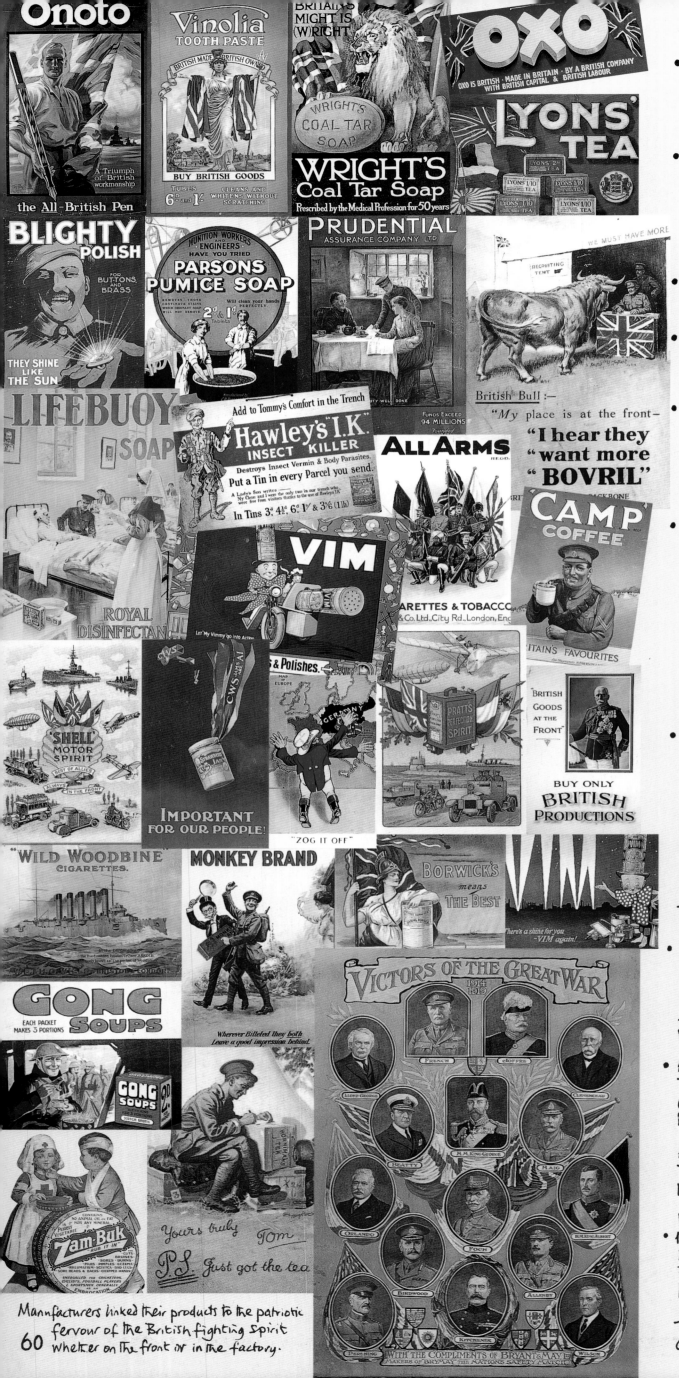

Manufacturers linked their products to the patriotic fervour of the British fighting spirit whether on the front or in the factory.

60

EVENTS of the 1910s

- **1910**
  Edward VII died
  Girl Guide movement founded
  Radio link enabled Dr Crippen to be captured a[t]
  General election gave Liberals and Tories 272 seats ea[ch]

- **1911**
  Sidney Street siege
  Coronation of George V
  House of Lords surrendered its veto
  World's first airmail, from Hendon to Windso[r]
  Woman's Weekly launched
  Amundsen beat Capt. Scott to South Pole

- **1912**
  Daily Herald launched
  Titanic sunk by iceberg on maiden voyage
  1,513 drowned

- **1913**
  Mrs Pankhurst on bomb charge
  First Chelsea Flower Show
  Woman's Own launched

- **1914**
  War on Germany declared (Aug. 4)
  Japan declared war on Germany (Aug 23)
  Income tax doubled to help pay for the war (N...)
  Death of Lord Roberts in France (Nov)
  German cruisers bomb Scarborough, Whitb[y]
  and Hartlepool: 127 killed (Dec)

- **1915**
  Zeppelins bomb Britain (Jan)
  Allies attack the Dardanelles (Feb)
  ANZAC, British and French fight for landing
  at Gallipoli (April)
  Germans use poison gas (April)
  Lusitania sunk by German submarine:
  1,195 drowned (May)
  VC awarded to aviator who shot down Zeppelin
  National registration required (Aug)
  Edith Cavell, a British nurse, shot on spy charge
  Allies retreat from Gallipoli disaster (Dec)

- **1916**
  Conscription Bill approved (Jan)
  German assault on Verdun (Feb)
  Easter uprising by Irish in Dublin (April)
  New 'Summer time' introduced (May)
  Naval battle of Jutland (May)
  Lord Kitchener drowned (June)
  Success by Canadians at Ypres (June)
  Somme offensive begun (July)
  Tanks used in battle on Somme (Sept)
  Two British Red Cross ships sunk by submarine (N...)
  Allies reject German peace overtures (Dec)

- **1917**
  Bread rationing introduced (Feb)
  Abdication of Tzar of Russia, Nicholas II (Ma...)
  USA enter the war (April)
  Aeroplane bombing reached London (June)
  Royal family renounce German titles;
  name changed to Windsor (June)

- **1918**
  Tank Week raised £138 million (March)
  Germans break through at Arras (March)
  Royal Flying Corps and Royal Naval Air Service
  combined to form Royal Air Force (Apr)
  Allies make 'final push' at Amiens (Aug)
  T.E. Lawrence led Arabs to Damascus (Oct)
  End of Great War (Nov. 11)
  1,260 civilians killed in Britain during war
  Kaiser fled to Holland

- **1919**
  League of Nations formed (Feb)
  First air service links London to Paris
  Influenza killed 150,000 in Britain (Feb)
  Alcock and Brown fly Atlantic non-stop
  Treaty of Versailles signed (June)
  German fleet scuttled at Scapa Flow (June)